LOVE POEMS

Emily Dickinson

PETER PAUPER PRESS, INC.
WHITE PLAINS • NEW YORK

Published by:
Peter Pauper Press, Inc.
202 Mamaroneck Avenue
White Plains, NY 10601
ISBN 0-88088-132-1
Printed in Hong Kong
5   4   3   2

A NOTE ON EMILY DICKINSON

WALT WHITMAN *of course: but after him our Emily Dickinson is the freshest, most unexpected voice in American poetry, and is surely the most affecting woman poet in English before Edna St. Vincent Millay.*

She was born in Amherst in 1830, lived there all her life, and died there in 1886. In that intellectual, pious, Victorian town she played the public role of an odd but devoted child and sister, thoughtful neighbor, sentimental spinster; but she also played out a bitter private role as disappointed lover.

On a rare journey out of Amherst she had met the one man who ignited her like a sulphur match on sandpaper. Her poems, taken literally, say that she became his lover; but it is any man's guess if this be fact or dream. We do know for fact that after some years of romance by correspondence, her friend made it clear that he could not or would not marry her.

Her poems tell how she suppressed her inner loss and hurt. Outwardly she grew only a bit more odd, more devoted, more sentimental — as might be expected of a sensitive maiden lady with big emotions and strange words to express them in.

For strange they were — "expressionist" we might call them, since feeling bursts out of the usual norms of grammar, rhyme and meter — so unconventional that it took half a century, and new free fashions in verse, to make them popular. And even then not entirely popular: for some must find the sentimentality of image slightly too quaint. But such criticism can never suppress the delight we feel at these brief, passionate, strange exclamations of a sensitive heart speaking to itself.

LOVE
POEMS

I HAD no time to hate, because
The grave would hinder me,
And life was not so ample I
Could finish enmity.

Nor had I time to love; but since
Some industry must be,
The little toil of love, I thought,
Was large enough for me.

THE OUTLET

MY RIVER runs to thee:
Blue sea, wilt welcome me?
My river waits reply.
Oh sea, look graciously!
I'll fetch thee brooks
From spotted nooks, —
Say, sea,
Take me!

If you were coming in the fall,
I'd brush the summer by
With half a smile and half a spurn,
As housewives do a fly.

If I could see you in a year,
I'd wind the months in balls,
And put them each in separate drawers,
Until their time befalls.

If only centuries delayed,
I'd count them on my hand,
Subtracting till my fingers dropped
Into Van Dieman's land.

If certain, when this life was out,
That yours and mine should be,
I'd toss it yonder like a rind,
And taste eternity.

But now, all ignorant of the length
Of time's uncertain wing,
It goads me, like the goblin bee,
That will not state its sting.

POSSESSION

Did the harebell loose her girdle
To the lover bee,
Would the bee the harebell hallow
Much as formerly?

Did the paradise, persuaded,
Yield the moat of pearl,
Would the Eden be an Eden,
Or the earl an earl?

I found the phrase to every thought
I ever had, but one;
And that defies me, — as a hand
Did try to chalk the sun

To races nurtured in the dark; —
How would your own begin?
Can blaze be done in cochineal,
Or moon in mazarin?

My cocoon tightens, colors tease,
I'm feeling for the air;
A dim capacity for wings
Degrades the dress I wear.

A power of butterfly must be
The aptitude to fly,
Meadows of majesty concedes
And easy sweeps of sky.

So I must baffle at the hint
And cipher at the sign,
And make much blunder, if at last
I take the clew divine.

THE LETTER

"Going to him! Happy letter! Tell him –
Tell him the page I didn't write;
Tell him I only said the syntax,
And left the verb and the pronoun out.

Tell him just how the fingers hurried,
Then how they waded slow, slow, slow;
And then you wished you had eyes in
        your pages,
So you could see what moved them so.

"Tell him it wasn't a practised writer,
You guessed from the way the sentence
        toiled;
You could hear the bodice tug, behind
        you,
As if it held but the might of a child;
You almost pitied it, you, it worked so.
Tell him — No, you may quibble there,
For it would split his heart to know it,
And then you and I were silenter.

"Tell him night finished before we
        finished,
And the old clock kept neighing 'day!'
And you got sleepy and begged to be
        ended —
What could it hinder so, to say?
Tell him just how she sealed you,
        cautious,
But if he ask where you are hid
Until to-morrow, — happy letter!
Gesture, coquette, and shake your head!"

THE LOVERS

THE rose did caper on her cheek,
Her bodice rose and fell,
Her pretty speech, like drunken men,
Did stagger pitiful.

Her fingers fumbled at her work, —
Her needle would not go;
What ailed so smart a little maid
It puzzled me to know,

Till opposite I spied a cheek
That bore another rose;
Just opposite, another speech
That like the drunkard goes;

A vest that, like the bodice, danced
To the immortal tune, —
Till those two troubled little clocks
Ticked softly into one.

THE way I read a letter's this:
'Tis first I lock the door,
And push it with my fingers next,
For transport it be sure.

And then I go the furthest off
To counteract a knock;
Then draw my little letter forth
And softly pick its lock.

Then, glancing narrow at the wall,
And narrow at the floor,
For firm conviction of a mouse
Not exorcised before,

Peruse how infinite I am
To — no one that you know!
And sigh for lack of heaven, — but not
The heaven the creeds bestow.

Our share of night to bear,
Our share of morning,
Our blank in bliss to fill,
Our blank in scorning.

Here a star, and there a star,
Some lose their way.
Here a mist, and there a mist,
Afterwards — day!

ALMOST

Within my reach!
I could have touched!
I might have chanced that way!
Soft sauntered through the village,
Sauntered as soft away!
So unsuspected violets
Within the fields lie low,
Too late for striving fingers
That passed, an hour ago.

'Tis so much joy! 'Tis so much joy!
If I should fail, what poverty!
And yet, as poor as I
Have ventured all upon a throw;
Have gained! Yes! Hesitated so
This side the victory!

Life is but life, and death but death!
Bliss is but bliss, and breath but breath!
And if, indeed, I fail,
At least to know the worst is sweet.
Defeat means nothing but defeat,
No drearier can prevail!

And if I gain, — Oh, gun at sea,
Oh, bells that in the steeples be,
Ah first repeat it slow!
For heaven is a different thing
Conjectured, and waked sudden in,
And might o'erwhelm me so!

OUT OF THE MORNING

WILL there really be a morning?
Is there such a thing as day?
Could I see it from the mountains
If I were as tall as they?

Has it feet like water-lilies?
Has it feathers like a bird?
Is it brought from famous countries
Of which I have never heard?

Oh, some scholar! Oh, some sailor!
Oh, some wise man from the skies!
Please to tell a little pilgrim
Where the place called morning lies!

WILD nights! Wild nights!
Were I with thee,
Wild nights should be
Our luxury!

Futile the winds
To a heart in port,
Done with the compass,
Done with the chart.

Rowing in Eden!
Ah! the sea!
Might I but moor
To-night in thee!

SUSPENSE

ELYSIUM is as far as to
The very nearest room,
If in that room a friend await
Felicity or doom.

What fortitude the soul contains,
That it can so endure
The accent of a coming foot,
The opening of a door!

ALTER? When the hills do.
Falter? When the sun
Question if his glory
Be the perfect one.
Surfeit? When the daffodil
Doth of the dew:
Even as herself, O friend!
I will of you!

THE TEST

I CAN wade grief,
Whole pools of it, —
I'm used to that.
But the least push of joy
Breaks up my feet,
And I tip — drunken.
Let no pebble smile,
'Twas the new liquor, —
That was all!

Power is only pain,
Stranded, through discipline,
Till weights will hang.
Give balm to giants,
And they'll wilt, like men.
Give Himmaleh, —
They'll carry him!

WHAT if I say I shall not wait?
What if I burst the fleshly gate
And pass, escaped, to thee?
What if I file this mortal off,
See where it hurt me, — that's enough, —
And wade in liberty?

They cannot take us any more, —
Dungeons may call, and guns implore,
Unmeaning now, to me,
As laughter was an hour ago,
Or laces, or a traveling show,
Or who died yesterday!

THE WHITE HEAT

DARE you see a soul at the white heat?
    Then crouch within the door.
Red is the fire's common tint;
    But when the vivid ore

Has sated flame's conditions,
    Its quivering substance plays
Without a color but the light
    Of unanointed blaze.

Least village boasts its blacksmith,
    Whose anvil's even din
Stands symbol for the finer forge
    That soundless tugs within,

Refining these impatient ores
    With hammer and with blaze,
Until the designated light
    Repudiate the forge.

TRIUMPHANT

Who never lost, are unprepared
A coronet to find;
Who never thirsted, flagons
And cooling tamarind.

Who never climbed the weary league —
Can such a foot explore
The purple territories
On Pizarro's shore?

How many legions overcome?
The emperor will say.
How many colors taken
On Revolution Day?

How many bullets bearest?
The royal scar hast thou?
Angels, write "Promoted"
On this soldier's brow!

SAVED

Of TRIBULATION these are they
Denoted by the white;
The spangled gowns, a lesser rank
Of victors designate.

All these did conquer; but the ones
Who overcame most times
Wear nothing commoner than snow,
No ornament but palms.

Surrender is a sort unknown
On this superior soil;
Defeat, an outgrown anguish,
Remembered as the mile

Our panting ankle barely gained
When night devoured the road;
But we stood whispering in the house,
And all we said was "Saved"!

THE CONTRACT

I GAVE myself to him,
And took himself for pay.
The solemn contract of a life
Was ratified this way.

The wealth might disappoint,
Myself a poorer prove
Than this great purchaser suspect,
The daily own of Love

Depreciate this vision;
But, till the merchant buy,
Still fable, in the isles of spice,
The subtle cargoes lie.

At least, 'tis mutual risk, —
Some found it mutual gain;
Sweet debt of Life, — each night to owe,
Insolvent, every noon.

The moon is distant from the sea,
And yet with amber hands
She leads him, docile as a boy,
Along appointed sands.

He never misses a degree;
Obedient to her eye,
He comes just so far toward the town,
Just so far goes away.

Oh, Signor, thine the amber hand,
And mine the distant sea, —
Obedient to the least command
Thine eyes impose on me.

I TASTE a liquor never brewed,
From tankards scooped in pearl;
Not all the vats upon the Rhine
Yield such an alcohol!

Inebriate of air am I,
And debauchee of dew,

Reeling, through endless summer days,
From inns of molten blue.

When landlords turn the drunken bee
Out of the foxglove's door,
When butterflies renounce their drams,
I shall but drink the more!

Till seraphs swing their snowy hats,
And saints to windows run,
To see the little tippler
Leaning against the sun!

I HAVE no life but this,
To lead it here;
Nor any death, but lest
Dispelled from there;

Nor tie to earths to come,
Nor action new,
Except through this extent,
The realm of you.

TRANSPLANTED

As IF some little Arctic flower,
Upon the polar hem,
Went wandering down the latitudes,
Until it puzzled came

To continents of summer,
To firmaments of sun,
To strange, bright crowds of flowers,
And birds of foreign tongue!

I say, as if this little flower
To Eden wandered in —
What then? Why, nothing, only
Your inference therefrom!

HUNGER

I HAD been hungry all the years;
My noon had come, to dine;
I, trembling, drew the table near,
And touched the curious wine

'Twas this on tables I had seen,
When turning, hungry, lone,
I looked in windows, for the wealth
I could not hope to own.

I did not know the ample bread,
'Twas so unlike the crumb
The birds and I had often shared
In nature's dining-room.

The plenty hurt me, 'twas so new, —
Myself felt ill and odd,
As berry of a mountain bush
Transplanted to the road.

Nor was I hungry; so I found
That hunger was a way
Of persons outside windows,
The entering takes away.

RENUNCIATION

THERE came a day at summer's full
Entirely for me;
I thought that such were for the saints,
Where revelations be.

The sun, as common, went abroad,
The flowers, accustomed, blew,
As if no soul the solstice passed
That maketh all things new.

The time was scarce profaned by speech;
The symbol of a word
Was needless, as at sacrament
The wardrobe of our Lord.

Each was to each the sealed church,
Permitted to commune this time,
Lest we too awkard show
At supper of the Lamb.

The hours slid fast, as hours will,
Clutched tight by greedy hands;
So faces on two decks look back,
Bound to opposing lands.

And so, when all the time had failed,
Without external sound,

Each bound the other's crucifix,
We gave no other bond.

Sufficient troth that we shall rise —
Deposed, at length, the grave —
To that new marriage, justified
Through Calvaries of Love!

OF ALL the souls that stand create
I have elected one.
When sense from spirit flies away,
And subterfuge is done;

When that which is and that which was
Apart, intrinsic, stand,
And this brief tragedy of flesh
Is shifted like a sand;

When figures show their royal front
And mists are carved away, —
Behold the atom I preferred
To all the lists of clay!

That I did always love,
I bring thee proof:
That till I loved
I did not love enough.

That I shall love alway,
I offer thee
That love is life,
And life hath immortality.

This, dost thou doubt, sweet?
Then have I
Nothing to show
But Calvary.

Doubt me, my dim companion!
Why, God would be content
With but a fraction of the love
Poured thee without a stint.
The whole of me, forever,
What more the woman can, —

Say quick, that I may dower thee
With last delight I own!

It cannot be my spirit,
For that was thine before;
I ceded all of dust I knew, —
What opulence the more
Had I, a humble maiden,
Whose farthest of degree
Was that she might,
Some distant heaven,
Dwell timidly with thee!

COME slowly, Eden!
Lips unused to thee,
Bashful, sip thy jasmines,
As the fainting bee,
Reaching late his flower,
Round her chamber hums,
Counts his nectars — enters,
And is lost in balms!

GOD permits industrious angels
Afternoons to play.
I met one, — forgot my school-mates,
All, for him, straightway.

God calls home the angels promptly
At the setting sun;
I missed mine. How dreary marbles,
After playing Crown!

HE PUT the belt around my life, —
I heard the buckle snap,
And turned away, imperial,
My lifetime folding up
Deliberate, as a duke would do
A kingdom's title-deed, —
Henceforth a dedicated sort,
A member of the cloud.

Yet not too far to come at call,
And do the little toils
That make the circuit of the rest,
And deal occasional smiles

To lives that stoop to notice mine
And kindly ask it in, —
Whose invitation, knew you not
For whom I must decline?

GOD gave a loaf to every bird,
But just a crumb to me;
I dare not eat it, though I starve, —
My poignant luxury
To own it, touch it, prove the feat
That made the pellet mine, —
Too happy in my sparrow chance
For ampler coveting.

It might be famine all around,
I could not miss an ear,
Such plenty smiles upon my board,
My garner shows so fair.
I wonder how the rich may feel, —
An Indiaman — an Earl?
I deem that I with but a crumb
Am sovereign of them all.

TRIUMPH

TRIUMPH may be of several kinds.
There's triumph in the room
When that old imperator, Death,
By faith is overcome.

There's triumph of the finer mind
When truth, affronted long,
Advances calm to her supreme,
Her God her only throng.

A triumph when temptation's bribe
Is slowly handed back,
One eye upon the heaven renounced
And one upon the rack.

Severer triumph, by himself,
Experienced, who can pass
Acquitted from the naked bar,
Jehovah's countenance!

I YEARS had been from home,
And now, before the door,
I dared not open, lest a face
I never saw before

Stare vacant into mine
And ask my business there.
My business, — just a life I left,
Was such still dwelling there?

I fumbled at my nerve,
I scanned the windows near;
The silence like an ocean rolled,
And broke against my ear.

I laughed a wooden laugh
That I could fear a door,
Who danger and the dead had faced,
But never quaked before.

I fitted to the latch
My hand, with trembling care,
Lest back the awful door should spring,
And leave me standing there.

I moved my fingers off
As cautiously as glass,
And held my ears, and like a thief
Fled gasping from the house.

I MEANT to have but modest needs,
Such as content, and heaven;
Within my income these could lie,
And life and I keep even.

But since the last included both,
It would suffice my prayer
But just for one to stipulate,
And grace would grant the pair.

And so, upon this wise I prayed, —
Great Spirit, give to me
A heaven not so large as yours,
But large enough for me.

A smile suffused Jehovah's face;
The cherubim withdrew;
Grave saints stole out to look at me,
And showed their dimples, too.

I left the place with all my might, —
My prayer away I threw;
The quiet ages picked it up,
And Judgment twinkled, too.

That one so honest be extant
As takes the tale for true
That "Whatsoever you shall ask,
Itself be given you."

But I, grown shrewder, scan the skies
With a suspicious air, —
As children, swindled for the first,
All swindlers be, infer.

APOCALYPSE

I'M WIFE; I've finished that,
That other state;
I'm Czar, I'm woman now:
It's safer so.

How odd the girl's life looks
Behind this soft eclipse!
I think that earth seems so
To those in heaven now.

This being comfort, then
That other kind was pain;
But why compare?
I'm wife! stop there!

THE WIFE

SHE rose to his requirement, dropped
The playthings of her life
To take the honorable work
Of woman and of wife.

If aught she missed in her new day
Of amplitude, or awe,
Or first prospective, or the gold
In using wore away,

It lay unmentioned, as the sea
Develops pearl and weed,
But only to himself is known
The fathoms they abide.

I BRING an unaccustomed wine
To lips long parching, next to mine,
And summon them to drink.

Crackling with fever, they essay;
I turn my brimming eyes away,
And come next hour to look.

The hands still hug the tardy glass;
The lips I would have cooled, alas!
Are so superfluous cold,

I would as soon attempt to warm
The bosoms where the frost has lain
Ages beneath the mould.

Some other thirsty there may be,
To whom this would have pointed me
Had it remained to speak,

And so I always bear the cup
If, haply, mine may be the drop
Some pilgrim thirst to slake, —

If, haply, any say to me,
"Unto the little, unto me,"
When I at last awake.

EXCEPT the heaven had come so near,
So seemed to choose my door,
The distance would not haunt me so;
I had not hoped before.

But just to hear the grace depart
I never thought to see,
Afflicts me with a double loss;
'Tis lost, and lost to me.

THE nearest dream recedes, unrealized.
    The heaven we chase
    Like the June bee
    Before the school-boy
    Invites the race;
Stoops to an easy clover —
Dips — evades — teases — deploys;
    Then to the royal clouds
    Lifts his light pinnace
    Heedless of the boy

Homesick for steadfast honey,
Staring, bewildered, at the mocking sky.

Ah! the bee flies not
That brews that rare variety.

EXCLUSION

THE soul selects her own society,
Then shuts the door;
On her divine majority
Obtrude no more.

Unmoved, she notes the chariot's pausing
At her low gate;
Unmoved, an emperor is kneeling
Upon her mat.

I've known her from an ample nation
Choose one;
Then close the valves of her attention
Like stone.

I GAINED it so,
    By climbing slow,
By catching at the twigs that grow
Between the bliss and me.
    It hung so high,
    As well the sky
    Attempts by strategy.

I said I gained it, —
    This was all.
Look, how I clutch it,
    Lest it fall,
And I a pauper go;
Unfitted by an instant's grace
For the contented beggar's face
I wore an hour ago.

LOVE'S BAPTISM

I'M CEDED, I've stopped being theirs;
The name they dropped upon my face
With water, in the country church,

Is finished using now,
And they can put it with my dolls,
My childhood, and the string of spools
I've finished threading too.

Baptized before without the choice,
But this time consciously, of grace
Unto supremest name,
Called to my full, the crescent dropped,
Existence's whole arc filled up
With one small diadem.

My second rank, too small the first,
Crowned, crowing on my father's breast,
A half unconscious queen;
But this time, adequate, erect,
With will to choose or to reject,
And I choose — just a throne.

SUCCESS

Success is counted sweetest
By those who ne'er succeed.
To comprehend a nectar
Requires sorest need.

Not one of all the purple host
Who took the flag to-day
Can tell the definition
So clear, of victory,

As he, defeated, dying,
On whose forbidden ear
The distant strains of triumph
Break, agonized and clear.

SIGHT

Before I got my eye put out,
I liked as well to see
As other creatures that have eyes,
And know no other way.

But were it told to me, to-day,
That I might have the sky
For mine, I tell you that my heart
Would split, for size of me.

The meadows mine, the mountains
    mine, —
All forests, stintless stars,
As much of noon as I could take
Between my finite eyes.

The motions of the dipping birds,
The lightning's jointed road,
For mine to look at when I liked, —
The news would strike me dead!

So, safer, guess, with just my soul
Upon the window-pane
Where other creatures put their eyes,
Incautious of the sun.

THE bustle in a house
The morning after death
Is solemnest of industries
Enacted upon earth, —

The sweeping up the heart,
And putting love away
We shall not want to use again
Until eternity.

THE SHELTER

THE body grows outside, —
The more convenient way, —
That if the spirit like to hide,
Its temple stands alway

Ajar, secure, inviting;
It never did betray
The soul that asked its shelter
In timid honesty.

THE DUEL

I TOOK my power in my hand
And went against the world;
'Twas not so much as David had,
But I was twice as bold.

I aimed my pebble, but myself
Was all the one that fell.
Was it Goliath was too large,
Or only I too small?

DAWN

WHEN night is almost done,
And sunrise grows so near
That we can touch the spaces,
It's time to smooth the hair

And get the dimples ready,
And wonder we could care
For that old faded midnight
That frightened but an hour.

ESCAPE

I NEVER hear the word "escape"
Without a quicker blood,
A sudden expectation,
A flying attitude.

I never hear of prisons broad
By soldiers battered down,
But I tug childish at my bars, —
Only to fail again!

BEQUEST

YOU left me, sweet, two legacies, —
A legacy of love
A Heavenly Father would content,
Had He the offer of;
You left me boundaries of pain
Capacious as the sea,
Between eternity and time,
Your consciousness and me.

THE MYSTERY OF PAIN

PAIN has an element of blank;
It cannot recollect
When it began, or if there were
A day when it was not.

It has no future but itself,
Its infinite realms contain
Its past, enlightened to perceive
New periods of pain.

DEED

A DEED knocks first at thought,
And then it knocks at will.
That is the manufacturing spot,
And will at home and well.

It then goes out an act,
Or is entombed so still
That only to the ear of God
Its doom is audible.

THE LOST JEWEL

I held a jewel in my fingers
And went to sleep.
The day was warm, and winds were
   prosy;
I said: " 'Twill keep."

I woke and chid my honest fingers, —
The gem was gone;
And now an amethyst remembrance
Is all I own.

I shall know why, when time is over,
And I have ceased to wonder why;
Christ will explain each separate anguish
In the fair schoolroom of the sky.

He will tell me what Peter promised,
And I, for wonder at his woe,
I shall forget the drop of anguish
That scalds me now, that scalds me now.

TILL THE END

I SHOULD not dare to leave my friend,
Because — because if he should die
While I was gone, and I — too late —
Should reach the heart that wanted me;

If I should disappoint the eyes
That hunted, hunted so, to see,
And could not bear to shut until
They "noticed" me — they noticed me;

If I should stab the patient faith
So sure I'd come — so sure I'd come,
It listening, listening, went to sleep
Telling my tardy name, —

My heart would wish it broke before,
Since breaking then, since breaking then,
Were useless as next morning's sun,
Where midnight frosts had lain!

To FIGHT aloud is very brave,
But gallanter, I know,
Who charge within the bosom,
The cavalry of woe.

Who win, and nations do not see,
Who fall, and none observe,
Whose dying eyes no country
Regards with patriot love.

We trust, in plumed procession,
For such the angels go,
Rank after rank, with even feet
And uniforms of snow.

WE PLAY at paste,
Till qualified for pearl,
Then drop the paste,
And deem ourself a fool.
The shapes, though, were similar,
And our new hands
Learned gem-tactics
Practicing sands.

LOST

I LOST a world the other day.
Has anybody found?
You'll know it by the row of stars
Around its forehead bound.

A rich man might not notice it;
Yet to my frugal eye
Of more esteem than ducats.
Oh, find it, sir, for me!

UNRETURNING

'Twas such a little, little boat
That toddled down the bay!
'Twas such a gallant, gallant sea
That beckoned it away!

'Twas such a greedy, greedy wave
That licked it from the coast;
Nor ever guessed the stately sails
My little craft was lost!

I DREADED that first robin so,
But he is mastered now,
And I'm accustomed to him grown, —
He hurts a little, though.

I thought if I could only live
Till that first shout got by,
Not all pianos in the woods
Had power to mangle me.

I dared not meet the daffodils,
For fear their yellow gown
Would pierce me with a fashion
So foreign to my own.

I wished the grass would hurry,
So when 'twas time to see,
He'd be too tall, the tallest one
Could stretch to look at me.

I could not bear the bees should come,
I wished they'd stay away
In those dim countries where they go:
What word had they for me?

They're here, though; not a creature
    failed,

No blossom stayed away
In gentle deference to me,
The Queen of Calvary.

Each one salutes me as he goes,
And I my childish plumes
Lift, in bereaved acknowledgment
Of their unthinking drums.

NOT in this world to see his face
Sounds long, until I read the place
Where this is said to be
But just the primer to a life
Unopened, rare, upon the shelf,
Clasped yet to him and me.

And yet, my primer suits me so
I would not choose a book to know
Than that, be sweeter wise;
Might some one else so learned be,
And leave me just my A B C,
Himself could have the skies.

I ASKED no other thing,
No other was denied.
I offered Being for it;
The mighty merchant smiled.

Brazil? He twirled a button,
Without a glance my way:
"But, madam, is there nothing else
That we can show to-day?"

REMORSE is memory awake,
Her companies astir, —
A presence of departed acts
At window and at door.

Its past set down before the soul,
And lighted with a match
Perusal to facilitate
Of its condensed despatch.

Remorse is cureless, — the disease
Not even God can heal;
For 'tis his institution, —
The complement of hell.

Afraid? Of whom am I afraid?
Not death; for who is he?
The porter of my father's lodge
As much abasheth me.

Of life? 'Twere odd I fear a thing
That comprehendeth me
In one or more existences
At Deity's decree.

Of resurrection? Is the east
Afraid to trust the morn
With her fastidious forehead?
As soon impeach my crown!

RESURGAM

At last to be identified!
At last, the lamps upon thy side,
The rest of life to see!
Past midnight, past the morning star!
Past sunrise! Ah! what leagues there are
Between our feet and day!

THE heart asks pleasure first,
And then, excuse from pain;
And then, those little anodynes
That deaden suffering;

And then, to go to sleep;
And then, if it should be
The will of its Inquistor;
The liberty to die.

EMANCIPATION

No RACK can torture me,
My soul's at liberty.
Behind this mortal bone
There knits a bolder one

You cannot prick with saw,
Nor rend with scymitar.
Two bodies therefore be;
Bind one, and one will flee.

The eagle of his nest
No easier divest
And gain the sky,
Than mayest thou,

Except thyself may be
Thine enemy;
Captivity is consciousness,
So's liberty.

At least to pray is left, is left.
O Jesus! in the air
I know not which thy chamber is, —
I'm knocking everywhere.

Thou stirrest earthquake in the south,
And maelstrom in the sea;
Say, Jesus Christ of Nazareth,
Hast thou no arm for me?

MINE

MINE by the right of the white election!
Mine by the royal seal!
Mine by the sign in the scarlet prison
Bars cannot conceal!

Mine, here in vision and in veto!
Mine, by the grave's repeal
Titled, confirmed, — delirious charter!
Mine, while the ages steal!

I NEVER lost as much but twice,
And that was in the sod;
Twice have I stood a beggar
Before the door of God!

Angels, twice descending
Reimbursed my store.
Burglar, banker, father,
I am poor once more!

I READ my sentence steadily,
Reviewed it with my eyes,
To see that I made no mistake
In its extremest clause, —
The date, and manner of the shame;
And then the pious form
That "God have mercy" on the soul
The jury voted him.

I made my soul familiar
With her extremity,
That at the last it should not be
A novel agony,
But she and Death, acquainted,
Meet tranquilly as friends,
Salute and pass without a hint —
And there the matter ends.